♡ You are His
Beloved Amy ♡

Blessings, ♡
♡ Wendy

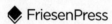

Suite 300 - 990 Fort St
Victoria, BC, V8V 3K2
Canada

www.friesenpress.com

Copyright © 2019 by Wendy Landin
First Edition — 2019

All rights reserved.

No part of this publication may be reproduced in any form, or by any means, electronic or mechanical, including photocopying, recording, or any information browsing, storage, or retrieval system, without permission in writing from FriesenPress.

ISBN

978-1-5255-4736-2 (Hardcover)
978-1-5255-4737-9 (Paperback)
978-1-5255-4738-6 (eBook)

1. RELIGION, BIBLICAL STUDIES

Distributed to the trade by The Ingram Book Company

"You are My Beloved"

DISCOVERING THE GRACE IN
IDENTITY & ORIGINAL DESIGN

WENDY LANDIN

Table of Contents

Foreword	vii
Introduction – Redemptive Gifting & Belovedness	xi
Day 1 The Permission and Empowerment of Grace	1
Day 2 So Arise Beloved…	15
Day 3 Yes, Simply Yes	27
Day 4 Legacy of Promise	41
Day 5 How Far Lord?	53
Day 6 Redemption Power	65
Day 7 God has the Best Ideas	77
Invitation	89
Afterword	91
Acknowledgments	93
About the Author	95

Foreword

I was thrilled to be asked, by my dear friend and mentor, to write a foreword for this book. This journey of discovery contains a depth of understanding of who God is and who we are that is refreshing, enlightening, and empowering. Wendy's Holy Spirit-inspired writing gets below the surface of Scripture passages and our understanding of self and of God. With each Scripture passage, Wendy introduces a perspective that I had never considered, seen, or understood in the past. This has led to a deeper revelation of the heart of God, the love of Jesus, and the fullness of the Holy Spirit. Every segment in this devotional is devoted to drawing us up and into the fullness of our identity as sons and daughters of the King. At the end of each reading, I found my spirit quickened in anticipation as a daughter of God, a re-ignited passionate love for Jesus, and a realignment with all things eternal. What I love about this devotional is that it exposes the limitations we have on our understandings and reminds us that our God is infinite. Therefore, there is always more for us; He is the God of "the more." There is always more revelation of who He is and who we are. This is exciting! I would encourage all readers to engage in this journey with a surrendered mind, body, soul, and spirit and to look forward with great anticipation for God to speak into the depths of your being.

Danae Henry
Revivalist and Educator

I have had the wonderful honor of doing ministry with Wendy. When she asked if I would read this; her first devotional that was to be published, I wholeheartedly jumped at the opportunity. You see Wendy has a gift of wisdom and discernment like very few I have ever been in the presence of. Wendy has a way of hearing the Father's voice and then transferring that into words on paper, a prayer or sound counsel. I am truly grateful to be a witness to such a beautiful facet of Jesus through my friend and ministry partner. This devotional is a beautiful way of seeing and hearing another dimension of our good Father through one of His steadfast and faithful servants. Thank you Wendy for this gift of a book.

Kimberly Mervyn
Director of Soul Care, The Holy Yoga Foundation

Introduction – Redemptive Gifting & Belovedness

Welcome to an adventure of delight, discovery, and design! I am so excited to share this time with you, to facilitate this space of grace, inviting the Lord to meet you right here and in His loving kindness, extending His invitation to draw closer to His heart. This experience is steeped in grace – "the permission to be exactly where you are; no shame, no condemnation as well as the invitation of His empowerment to arise to the more." He is so faithful.

My intention with this book is for us to experience our Lord in a new way, a way that is personal, intimate, and empowering. May each chapter not only draw us closer to His heart, but also awaken a freedom cry from the depths of our subdued souls.

Our Christian journeys are steeped in hope. We are going to adventure into the opportunity and promises made from the moment of design, the moment of His love for you, the invitation to "the more" in Christ. We are going to courageously look at our hearts through Kingdom glasses and see the beauty He sees.

This reflective devotional is the invitation to draw deeper, to catch His breath and then catch yours, to take an account of your own inner workings to see God's fingerprints of design all over them and to steep in the truth that you are His Beloved. "For the Holy Spirit makes God's fatherhood real to us as he whispers into our innermost being, 'You are God's beloved child'" Romans 8:16 TPT.

My journey with this devotional came to be as I spent one year studying redemptive gifting, taught by the work of Arthur Burk. I am fascinated by how we are all wired; the differences and similarities, the complexities as well as the simplicities, the depths and the overall potential of every single person – no exceptions. I am also profoundly drawn to take a deeper look behind the actions, the patterns, the choices, and the beliefs. We are all designed in love, by love, for love, so with this truth at the forefront of each chapter, we can begin to see ourselves and others through wonder of God's design; His image woven within our very DNA. We are His Beloved.

From the beginning of time, God was intentional about sharing His love, His fullness, His everything with His crowning creation – mankind. We will be exploring these truths as they are woven within each chapter.

All throughout Scripture it speaks of fulfillments of gifts. The phrase "redemptive gifting" was new to me, but I now understand gifting as; redemptive gifts, Holy Spirit-anointed gifts, and the offices of gifts. As you read this you may have layers of truth and understanding to add to it, but I want to invite you to a moment of simple trust as the Holy Spirit wants to reveal His heart for us.

Trust that He will bring us into all truth. May we journey on with wide-open hearts as the Lord speaks.

Redemptive gifting is a description of the image of God, the character of God, and the pieces of Himself that He shares with each person ever born. "So God created mankind in His own image, in the image of God He created them; male and female He created them." Genesis 1:27

This creation of man and woman did not stop at Adam and Eve – it says He created mankind, male and female and all peoples over all time. He went even further than the gift of creation for throughout mankind; He made man in His image. Pausing here for a moment…in His image. He means His own character, His heart, His image in each one of us, within our very DNA…That should stop each of us in our tracks. Meditating on this truth can truly be a new pair of lenses to view ourselves and for our relational view and world view.

The second is Holy Spirit-anointed gifts. They are gifts we receive when we choose Christ as Lord and saviour and therefore the Holy Spirit dwells within us. These gifts are then added beautifully to our original design; our redemptive gifting.

The third is primary-leadership anointing, which is for everyone in Christ.

This is a very basic description of the three and a lifetime of study would still not be enough time to understand the fullness of each gift and fulfillment of application.

The following devotional work is my humble attempt to speak to the ears of the seven redemptive gifts; the character gifts, the reflections of God's image. From the teaching of Arthur Burk it is clear that the name of each gift does not necessarily explain the virtues of each gift. These are described as Prophet, Servant, Teacher, Exhorter, Giver, Ruler, and Mercy. This work does not define these gifts in their fullness yet each devotional is written with an aspect of each specific gift in mind.

As I said, redemptive gifts are our base character personality (plus so much more). They are our hard wiring. They are our original way of thinking, doing, being, etc. All seven gifts can be represented and when hearing the same information, it will be originally perceived in seven different ways. This is our original design, our redemptive gifting working via perception. (Then we add our uniqueness to this for another layer of perception – that's another devotional for another day.) It takes maturing and revelation for each one of us to hear or see differently than ourselves. Our belovedness creates the capacity to do just that.

Wonderfully, Jesus is all seven gifts, He is the fullness of the image of God as He is God. As we are in relationship with Him, as we have submitted, surrendered, and released our life to Him as our Lord and saviour, He then gives us the Holy Spirit to dwell within us. The Holy Spirit then matures us in His image, to procure more of our hearts, minds, souls, and strength to be more like Him. Therefore, as much as each devotional is designed with specific gifts in mind, these truths can be heard by each one of us as Christ is maturing us in all seven of the redemptive gifts.

This word is designed to be of great encouragement and a tool to draw each of us closer to the fullness of God and who He created us to be. May each day find you postured at the foot of His throne, steeped in His presence, receiving love beyond measure, and moving from glory to glory into the fullness of your birthright, your inheritance. May this be a Genesis experience for each of us as He begins and enlightens a new thing within us. May it also be a Revelation experience as He takes us deeper and deeper until His story is complete in each one of us. God bless you richly as you are His Beloved.

[17]Every good and perfect gift is from above, coming down from the Father of the heavenly lights, who does not change like shifting shadows. [18] He chose to give us birth through the word of truth that we might be a kind of first fruits of all he created (James 1, NIV).

Beloved, I invite you to sit with the Lord in a space of wonder as you read. To reflect and explore your own experience; taking time to journal, to pray, to worship. Also to come back and reread again and again, each time exploring with the Lord, as there are beautiful layers of love and revelation to discover.

I am praying for you. <3

Blessing, Wendy

Day 1

The Permission and Empowerment of Grace

Today is a perfect day to begin with your cup filled with a steaming blend of your favorite goodness, a comfy chair, and time set apart for and with the Lord.

So settle in, chosen one. God has much for us today.

Matthew 18:21-35

Peter: [21] Lord, when someone has sinned against me, how many times ought I forgive him? Once? Twice? As many as seven times?

Jesus: [22] You must forgive not seven times, but seventy times seven. [23] If you want to understand the Kingdom of Heaven, think about a king who wanted to settle accounts with his servants. [24] Just as the king began to get his accounts in order, his assistants called his attention to a slave who owed a huge sum to him – what a laborer might make in 500 lifetimes. [25] The slave, maybe an embezzler, had no way to make restitution, so the king ordered that he, his wife, their children, and everything the family owned be sold on the auction block; the proceeds from the slave sale would go toward paying back the king. [26] Upon hearing this judgment, the slave fell down, prostrated himself before the king, and begged for mercy: "Have mercy on me, and I will somehow pay you everything." [27] The king was moved by the pathos of the situation, so indeed he took pity on the servant, told him to stand up, and then forgave the debt.

[28] But the slave went and found a friend, another slave, who owed him about a hundred days' wages. "Pay me back that money," shouted the slave, throttling his friend and shaking him with threats and violence. [29] The slave's friend fell down prostrate and begged for mercy: "Have mercy on me, and I will somehow pay you everything." [30] But the first slave cackled and was hard-hearted and refused to hear his friend's plea. He found a magistrate and had his friend thrown into prison "where," he said, "you will sit until you can pay me back." [31] The other servants saw what was going on. They were upset, so they went to the king and told him everything that had happened.

[32] The king summoned the slave, the one who had owed so much money, the one whose debt the king had forgiven. The king was livid. "You slovenly scum," he said, seething with anger. "You begged me to forgive your debt, and I did. [33] What would be the faithful response to such latitude and generosity? Surely you should have shown the same charity to a friend who was in your debt."

[34] The king turned over the unmerciful slave to his brigade of torturers, and they had their way with him until he should pay his whole debt. [35] And that is what My Father in Heaven will do to you, unless you forgive each of your brothers and each of your sisters from the very cockles of your heart.

When I first read this passage I see a parable with a distinct pattern of entitlement, debt, judgement, mercy, entitlement, debt, judgement …mercy?? Where is the mercy? God's laws always follow His order of natural law and this pattern looks unfinished, broken, hopeless, and works-orientated versus merciful. It finished with torture…how is that merciful? Notice with me that this pattern is also one of man's sin nature – entitlement, debt repayment, judgement from person to person – and then in His redemption the pattern finishes with His extension of mercy. So where is His extension of mercy in torture???

Ahhh, this is where God in all His GODness does a merciful act, a life filled with grace and kindness if only the servant will see it.

Have you ever had a debt you could not pay, had no hope of paying, and had no possible retribution to satisfy the debt owed?

As much as we think of money as our largest debt source, we can easily answer these questions by looking at the price Jesus paid on the cross for our sin. We had no possible way to pay for that debt, we couldn't and can't work hard enough, give big enough, sacrifice long enough, or serve joyfully enough. There is simply no human way, in our own strength to pay the debt for our sin.

God knew this from the beginning. He made it this way, He already had a plan of reconciliation; it is Jesus. Jesus knew this plan from the beginning of time and still He agreed to it. This is what love looks like, this is what mercy looks like, grace abounding. A free gift to be reconciled to the father through the sacrifice of His son Jesus. A price we don't have to pay when we receive the free gift of mercy. We simply have to ask. Just like the servant in the parable we fall at our King's feet and ask for mercy. "[27] The king was moved by the pathos of the situation, so indeed he took pity on the servant, told him to stand up, and then forgave the debt."

He forgave the massive debt.

The King's act of mercy is so powerful, freeing, and an indescribable release from an irreconcilable debt. That is what Jesus did on the cross. He not only made a way to the Father, but He completely broke the chains of bondage to the previous debt. There was no payment plan, there was no community service plan, there was no bond-servant plan, and there was no demand for the first child to be given to repay-plan. It was a once and for all forgiveness plan, a release from ever coming back to claim debts previously owed. It was finished.

The amazing fact that Jesus/the King does this so willingly for all those who ask is perhaps where our human way of thinking, justifying, and understanding gets tripped up.

Familiar conversations we may have with ourselves might be: How is complete forgiveness possible? Did He forget what I have done? I don't deserve complete forgiveness; if God honestly knows who I am, then this promise isn't for me. I am such a hypocrite; if people knew the true me they wouldn't ever come to Jesus. I need to look, be, and act good enough so that people see the grace Jesus has promised. I really need to protect God – even if I am not good enough, I can show people that God made my life perfect and therefore He is good. I don't understand, If God knows how much they hurt me, then how can he forgive them? Don't we need to be good enough? Don't I need to strive for angelic replication? Don't I need to unselfishly serve everyone all the time? Maybe if I just remember everything, if I give more, if I say it better, if I only show the good stuff, if I just try harder, if I could just suffer for the gospel a bit deeper…God deserves that much, RIGHT?????

How often we have asked these questions? Notice with me that these familiar conversations are inherently dependent on ourselves, our performance, our ability, our striving or even white knuckling our lives into submission. Oh beloved, cry mercy.

God answers these questions with Isaiah 55:9 "As the Heavens are higher than the Earth, so are my ways higher than your ways and my thoughts than your thoughts." Thank goodness…we can exhale. Let's explore together His higher ways and thoughts.

The king told the servant to STAND up and He then forgave the debt. The king told him to stand up, why is that important? I am sure there is more than one reason for this but one of them is that forgiveness requires participation, a willingness to have our internal posture transformed. Perhaps symbolically and literally, standing up gives the servant an opportunity to fully embrace the gift, to look the king in the eyes, to perhaps have open hands to receive and also to symbolically place down the emotional burden he would have been carrying. He had the servant come off the floor from his begging posture to a posture of availability to fully receive the grace given. Yet still the servant left the king's presence and quickly forgot as he pursued a fellow slave to repay a much smaller debt owed.

The parable continues to say the first servant sought out a fellow servant to make good on a debt owed. Understandably, debt repayment is expected. We each have responsibility to repay each other for what we owe. The debt between fellow servants was much smaller than the debt to the king but it still equalled a hundred-days' wages. It is understandable (if we put ourselves in his shoes) that he would "need" this money, that he and his family deserved that money. He had worked hard for that money, and after all he had been gracious enough to lend it to his fellow servant. Why shouldn't he get that money back? Culturally it was fair to demand payment and force bondage (a.k.a. jail), until full payment was received. He was justifiably and understandably right when demanding payment and it was fully within his own rights to have his fellow servant thrown in jail. So why was there a big deal made of this action for repayment? It was his own personal right…right??

Observe with me that the king also deserved, was entitled to, had rights, was qualified, and justified and that it would have been culturally fair to throw the servant and his family in jail or sold, but the king CHOSE grace, he CHOSE mercy above his own rights, his justifications, his entitlements, and what he knew he deserved. That choice allowed for a river of grace to flow, and created an opportunity and empowerment to release the servant from an exponential debt owed.

The problem comes when the reality of the grace received by the servant was not internally redemptive; there was no internal transformation. It says the servant had hardened his heart. Servant #1 not only received a gift beyond measure, grace beyond description, and mercy from all bondage, but he also received an opportunity to allow those truths to change his heart, mind, soul, and strength. Not by what he could do but by receiving the fullness of the grace given. The grace given was not only permission to be himself but also the invitation and empowerment to be even more than his bonded self.

The parable continues with the hardened servant being held accountable for his actions. Being brought before the king who said, [32] "You begged me to forgive your debt, and I did. [33] What would be the faithful response to such latitude and generosity? Surely you should have shown the same charity to a friend who was in your debt."

[34] The king turned over the unmerciful slave to his brigade of torturers, and they had their way with him until he should pay his whole debt.[35] And that is what My Father in heaven will do to you, unless you forgive each of your brothers and each of your sisters from the very cockles of your heart.

This is the part of the parable that begs the question… Where is the mercy? Torture…really? Jail…really? How can he pay for anything while being tortured? Doesn't that make him unavailable? God the King, did this??

Ah beloved, this is where revelation and mercy collide. Servant #1 was turned over to his torturers, who had their way with him until such time that this servant could repay the debt owed.

Throughout the parable it is repeated three times that servant #1's debt is forgiven. He didn't owe anything anymore, he had nothing to repay, he had no restitution owing to the king, yet the king knew full well that the servant owed him nothing and demanded "payment."

The king needed, wanted, desired beyond measure for the servant to understand the fullness of forgiveness. The king knew he had hardened his heart for the fruit of unforgiveness had proven it. The king desperately needed servant #1 to see, know, fully receive, and claim the gift of forgiveness, grace, and mercy that he had been given. He allowed Servant #1 to be turned over to his torturers.

How much torture do we experience mentally, emotionally, spiritually, and physically when we try so hard to pay for or earn the gift of mercy and grace? How often do we harden our hearts and participate with the bondage of unforgiveness? Reliving and replaying pain? Planning harsh conversations and righteous vengeance? Protecting ourselves by emotionally retreating to a place of internal isolation and mistrust? By hurting those around us before they can hurt us? Each one is willing participation with our torturers. How long do we stay in the grips of our torturers before we realize we don't owe ANYTHING? Our King has cancelled our debt. He paid for it himself. He has released us from having to repay and replay the bondage of our past. From His grace we have the empowerment to not stay in the grip of our tortures. He has broken the chains. He has forgiven our debt.

The servant needed to see his own freedom, his own choice, and his own participation. He was not a victim to the unjust, and he always had a choice; for he had been forgiven, the chains had been broken, and he was released from the cost. The resistant servant simply had to recognize he didn't owe anything. It was this servant who needed to see the fullness of the gift of mercy; to see the freedom he had been given. It was this servant who needed to say no to the torture, the bondage, and the grips of his past. He simply had to participate with the grace he had been given, not by his own strength, but by the empowerment of freedom he had already received from his king.

When we compare the vast debt we owe to the justifiable debt owed to us, it then becomes possible to choose to forgive those who owe us because we now fully embrace the gift of forgiveness that we have received. From our King's grace we can extend grace to much lesser debts even when we may be entitled, and payment for such debts is justified, deserved, merited, and within our rights.

The Lord does not abandon us with no choice for freedom. He already provided a way out through His gift of mercy, grace, and forgiveness. Jesus paid the price once and for all. A free gift.

The gift of grace is twofold; the Lord meets us right where we are. He is never offended by us and then with love, He invites us to not stay there. He comes to us and invites us to draw up and out with Him. He invites and empowers us to stand.

Let's challenge the servant #1 in each one of us, who quickly forgets the fullness of forgiveness, grace, and mercy. The love of God's grace empowers us to forgive ourselves and those who owe us. Not of our own merit but by His grace can we forgive. Nothing compares to the vast debt that we owe, it nailed Jesus to the cross.

This parable has a beautiful pattern of entitlement, debt, judgement, mercy, entitlement, debt, judgement, and yes, mercy. For God does not break the natural laws He put in place from the beginning. He will always meet us right where we are and extend the invitation and empowerment to not stay there. He will always finish what He has started and it will always be steeped in mercy, grace, and forgiveness.

Let us not forget the fullness of the gift we have received, walking in the freedom from our bondage, and forgiving those with lesser debts. "For it is by grace you have been saved, through faith and this not from yourselves, it is a Gift from God" (Ephesians 2:8).

Thank you, Jesus, for taking the price for my debt to the cross with you. Give me a fresh understanding of this profound truth today. Let me hear through Kingdom ears your voice afresh. Challenge and bring your revelation to my heart, mind, soul, and strength; showing me my choices. I choose your empowering grace to stand and receive your forgiveness, to say no to my torturers and claim your truth. I am forgiven, I am free, I am released from my past bondage.

In Jesus's name I say no to my own participation with conditional thinking and believing and receive the fullness of unconditional grace and mercy. Today I choose you, your grace, and to extend that grace to others, forgiving those who don't deserve it, just as I didn't. Thank you for showing me your Kingdom perspective, Lord. I choose you today – thank you for choosing me from the beginning. I love you. In Jesus' name.

References;
The Voice Bible
NIV Bible
Commentary from Charles R. Wale Jr.'s voice recording on the prophet; Arthur Burk

Day 2

So Arise Beloved...

Oh how fun for the Lord to peel back the curtains and reveal another layer of His heart, His character, and His design in each one of us. This passage in Luke has a hidden treasure.

So get comfy, beloved. Settle in, and let's journey in grace, mercy, and the fullness of God's goodness.

Luke 14:7-11

⁷⁻⁹ He went on to tell a story to the guests around the table. Noticing how each had tried to elbow into the place of honor, he said, "When someone invites you to dinner, don't take the place of honor. Somebody more important than you might have been invited by the host. Then he'll come and call out in front of everybody, "You're in the wrong place. The place of honor belongs to this man." Red-faced, you'll have to make your way to the very last table, the only place left.

¹⁰⁻¹¹ When you're invited to dinner, go and sit at the last place. Then when the host comes he may very well say, "Friend, come up to the front." That will give the dinner guests something to talk about. What I'm saying is, If you walk around with your nose in the air, you're going to end up flat on your face. But if you're content to be simply yourself, you will become more than yourself."

Throughout Luke 14 is very clear on the importance of humbling ourselves. He presents a few examples of how ego can look in each one of us, how God handles it, and also how He feels about us. Let's take a look at the most evident presence of ego and how God speaks to this and then let's visit the example of ego that is notably more subtle.

Within the first teaching, the parable paints two scenes. The beginning of the parable shows if we don't choose humility willingly, then in the fullness of his Love God will give us opportunity to learn it. Luke warns in this passage that when we assume or are presumptuous, when our ego takes us to the head tables of our lives, then we will be asked to move to make space for the true person of honour. We will be red-faced, embarrassed and humiliated before all witnesses. We will have to take the last seat available at the last table. We all know this experience; the moment when God in his true love for us doesn't leave us in our public ego. He provides everything we need to be humbled and return our hearts back to him.

Historically, the last table was for the kitchen help, the servants of the feasts, the ones who made this feast possible without any fanfare for themselves. They each knew the value of their position in the evening; the value they brought to the event, and therefore they joyfully served. In my own imagination (whether historically applicable or not) I picture a group of kitchen help seated, while on their break, with no competitive aspirations against those around them. I see them laughing amongst themselves as they enjoy their food, the company, and the pride of a job well done. Enjoying their moment before they are called back to work for the cleanup portion of the evening. For the servant heart much joy comes from creating a space, a feast, a celebration for others to truly enjoy the host's goodness. There is joy in serving, there is fulfillment in providing for others, and there is purpose in establishing the scene for someone else to flourish. There is contentment in the unseen foundations, service, and provisions given for others.

I imagine their surprise when a guest from the party, a person with great influence, although not the most powerful in the room, is then seated at their table. Bringing with him his public humiliation and the powerful presence of his ego being dethroned. I can imagine their surprise and discomfort over what to do or say next. It's easy to feel the awkward climate around this table. Scenario #1 is a difficult way to learn humility.

Also presented in this parable is Scenario #2; *"When you're invited to dinner, go and sit at the last place."*

He wants us to start at the last table. Not simply physically but from the heart. A servant-positioning in the heart makes no room for ego. Therefore, no matter their societal, ministerial, or professional stations in life, their presence at the servants' table would "feel" no different than if they were positioned at the kitchen. I now picture this new scene…a humble, willing person now comes and joins the dinner table of the kitchen help. The conversations are now inclusive and joyful, and the presence of humility is blessing their table. There wouldn't be a separation of stations, of value, of importance to the feast or the host; the heart of each person at the table has a clear understanding of who they are.

This is where the parable takes hidden treasures and splays them open for the beautiful servant heart to receive. Opportunity #2, the notably more subtle example…

The parable continues with, *"When you're invited to dinner, go and sit at the last place. Then when the host comes he may very well say, 'Friend, come up to the front.' That will give the dinner guests something to talk about. What I'm saying is, If you walk around with your nose in the air, you're going to end up flat on your face. But if you're content to be simply yourself, you will become more than yourself."*

The passage says the host may then come and say, "Friend come to the front." This invitation will get one of two reactions and the hidden treasure that God can splay open for each one of us is simply this… this may not sound like the public ego we quickly understand but it is ego none the less.

When our host comes to the table to invite us our reaction is either; #1, the trusting of the host's call to be equipped to be moved to the front or; #2, fear and denying the invitation to arise. Oh beloved, how often do we have this conversation with our Lord? It is either; "Lord I trust you, I will follow you," OR "Lord I am not doing that." How often do we disqualify ourselves based on fear and justifying our God-given weaknesses? How quickly we can hear ourselves say… "I don't know how, it's too risky." "I am not made for that, you have me confused for someone else." "I am happy doing what I am doing." "Can't you see I am serving you from this station in my life, Lord?" "I am made for serving in the background, not up front." "I make a difference right here." "I wouldn't know what to say, what to do, where to go, how to do it, there are lots of people made for the spotlight, not me. I will stay here Lord." "Lord, I know all the people at my table, I am accepted here, I feel my belonging here, I am a significant part of this team here Lord, I can't leave." We all have these conversations with the Lord as He woos us to himself. In the meantime, we grow to see that these conversations are self-preserving and therefore are based in our ego as well. This expression of ego may not elbow its way to the publicly-honoured head tables but it does elbow its way to the throne of our own hearts. How quickly we may deny the invitation the Lord gives to us; to move us to a different seat, a different table, a place He has created for us to fill, a land He has made a way for us to dwell in, inviting us into a new dream, or a new focus. The host is asking us to willingly step down from the exalted place of honour in our own lives, so that Jesus, the one more honourable, can have that seat. He is asking our humbled selves to willingly take the trusting, surrendered place at the last table.

The beauty of faith, of surrendering the throne of our hearts to the Lord himself, is that He stays with us. He equips, empowers, prepares, and goes before us to fulfill the birthright that He bestowed. He desires our devotion, our service, our love, and commitment to the station where He has placed us and also that we be willing to follow His invitation when it comes, to arise and follow Him to another place. The Lord takes away our inadequacy and gives us His adequacy. It's because of how good He is that we can rise up and be who we are created to be. He has good plans and purposes, therefore we do not need to fear when He extends the invitation to follow and to trust him fully.

Looking at one of the great servants, Moses, we see this journey of humility in the most dynamic expression. God made this beautiful servant man with all his strengths and his weaknesses so that God's glory could be exalted in the fullest life Moses could possibly live out. With some life behind him we see Moses; a man in hiding, this man with deep personal woundedness, one who desired a good life, a quiet life, a hidden life. Moses, a servant to all he encountered throughout his life. He did not aspire to the places of public honour; he didn't elbow his way through the castle to the public thrones. He didn't do all he could do to draw exaltation, praise, and position even though he could have.

Here is Moses going from slavery roots to an exalted life purely because of his family status; to a man on the run with a broken, fear-filled heart; onto becoming a man who profoundly changed history.

Let's fast forward into Moses's life when God met him in the desert and spoke to him through the burning bush. God knew Moses, he knew Moses better than Moses knew Moses.

God had come over to Moses' table and invited him to follow him, to come to another table, to enter a new conversation, a new station in life, and to trust Him fully as God would equip him as he went. What was Moses's response? "Not me Lord, you must mean someone else. Who am I? I don't know what to say, I am not eloquent. I don't want to, please send someone else to do it." Moses, one of the greatest in the word of God, had the same kind of conversations we have with the Lord. This is reassuring – that God fully knows the heart behind these conversations, because let's look at what God does next. He calls Moses out on who is seated as the Lord of his own heart. He asks him to move off this seat for there is one more honourable. As Moses humbles his heart, trusting the Lord fully, the Lord does a beautiful thing.

If Moses could have freed the slaves on his own, then he would have done it when he was in a public position to do it. Strengths are not what God uses here. God uses Moses's fears and his disqualifications to establish his dependence on the Lord. From that dependency comes the greatest exodus of God's people leaving their bondage.

When Moses arose from his table, God provided everything needed to accomplish the calling on his life. He gave him a team, signs and wonders, words of influence, and courage, direction, and timing. To top it all off, God gave Moses the anointing to move nature for God's glory.

The highlighted part of the parable concludes with, *"But if you're content to be simply yourself, you will become more than yourself."* This is the part, beloved, that should blow us back into our comfy chairs. God doesn't ask us to be someone else. He says, here we are to be simply ourselves. Only then can we become more than ourselves.

We are "simply ourselves" *when* Jesus is enthroned on our hearts. Being simply ourselves *is* the position of fully humble, fully accepting, and fully content with who we are created to be; our truest selves without the elbowing, the striving, the needing of position, power, or influence. Our authentic selves have no need to play small or hold back in fear. It is the fullness of who God made us with the humble heart to receive the invitation to arise and to follow. Only then do "we become more than ourselves."

It is in each one of us to arise to His calling, to follow wholeheartedly into places of unknown, to find the willingness to join Him at another table, knowing He is already there. The becoming more of ourselves in not in our own strength, it is the empowering of the Holy Spirit. Emerging from loving the Lord, obedience to arise is possible.

We see in Moses's example that God has powerful plans for servant hearts. Humbly participating with all the Lord is doing, not for our own glory but for the Lord's glory to be displayed. Following in pure dependency with Holy Spirit-courage and boldness.

We also see in Moses's story an anointing that is unprecedented. Through the anointing on Moses's servant heart, he was entrusted with authority over the natural world. With a word and raising of his arm, a sea opened up, friends. This man went from faithfully tending sheep to separating a sea to free thousands…God took Moses' servant heart; his humble heart, and He exalted Moses among the nations. Through God's plan and purposes for

Moses, God's people gained a freedom they did not know was possible.

When the Lord came to the table, Moses answered the invitation to arise, trusting the Lord's leadership, and doing it afraid, walking in obedience, staying humble through all signs and wonders, and walking out with Holy Spirit-courage. It was then that Moses, in his *contentment to be himself*, discovered what it truly meant to *"become more than himself."*

The calling is here, the invitation has been given…

Humbly arise, beloved, and follow your loving God to the table at which He asks you to join Him. Fix your eyes on the Lord and He will perform many signs and wonders. Step into the fullness of the anointing He has on you; you too will part vast passages of impossibility, making a way for salvation, freedom, and the crumbling of the enemy around you. The Holy Spirit is waiting to tell you what to say, when to say it, where to go, how to do it, and to fully walk out all He has for you. Not by our own strength do we need to elbow our way or position ourselves comfortably, but by His equipping we have seas to part. The Lord is so for you, extending His loving invitation for His glory to shine out through your life. So arise, beloved.

Lord, forgive me for my ego. Whether it is loud or quiet, it de-throned you. With your grace and mercy I ask you to take the place on the throne of my heart. Reign in your power, might, and abounding love. With your Holy Spirit-courage I say yes. Yes to the invitation to arise, to the invitation to another table, another conversation, and a deeper intimacy with you, Lord.

I say yes to the fullness of dependence I have on you. I fully surrender the throne of my heart to all that you are. I desire to know you in the deep spaces within myself, expressing the fullness of your truth that I am more IN you, and you have a very specific fulfillment for me personally to satisfy throughout my life here.

Lord, I am trusting you fully today, surrendering the throne of my heart, knowing your promises of completion, presence, and provision are without compromise. With humble faith I arise.

Praise you, Lord, from glory to glory, in Jesus's name.

---

*References;
The Message Bible and NIV Bible
Commentary from Charles R. Wale Jr.'s voice recording on the servant; Arthur Burk

Day 3

Yes, Simply Yes

Richness flows from being hidden in Christ. For it is Him who brings wonder and revelation, and revelation is only the beginning of the new thing He is doing.

Holy Spirit gives us your ears to hear the fullness of your profound love for us this day.

Oh beloved, the Lord of the whole universe is with you, calling your name. He loves you beyond measure and speaks His heart for you today. Snuggle in. He is so good.

The Lord Calls Samuel

[3] The boy, Samuel, ministered before the Lord under Eli. In those days, the word of the Lord was rare; there were not many visions.

² One night, Eli, whose eyes were becoming so weak that he could barely see, was lying down in his usual place. ³ The Lamp of God had not yet gone out, and Samuel was lying down in the house of the Lord, where the Ark of God was. ⁴ Then the Lord called Samuel.

Samuel answered, "Here I am." ⁵ And he ran to Eli and said, "Here I am; you called me."

But Eli said, "I did not call; go back and lie down." So he went and lay down.

⁶ Again the Lord called, "Samuel." And Samuel got up and went to Eli and said, "Here I am; you called me."

"My son," Eli said, "I did not call; go back and lie down."

⁷ Now Samuel did not yet know the Lord: The word of the Lord had not yet been revealed to him.

⁸ A third time the Lord called, "Samuel." And Samuel got up and went to Eli and said, "Here I am; you called me."

Then Eli realized that the Lord was calling the boy. ⁹ So Eli told Samuel, "Go and lie down, and if he calls you, say, 'Speak, Lord, for your servant is listening.'" So Samuel went and lay down in his place.

¹⁰ The Lord came and stood there, calling as at the other times, "Samuel. Samuel."

Then Samuel said, "Speak, for your servant is listening."

¹¹ And the Lord said to Samuel: "See, I am about to do something in Israel that will make the ears of everyone who hears about it tingle.¹² At that time I will carry out against Eli everything I spoke against his family – from beginning to end. ¹³ For I told him that I would judge his family forever because of the sin he knew about; his

sons blasphemed God,[a] and he failed to restrain them. ¹⁴ Therefore I swore to the house of Eli, 'The guilt of Eli's house will never be atoned for by sacrifice or offering.'"

¹⁵ Samuel lay down until morning and then opened the doors of the house of the Lord. He was afraid to tell Eli the vision, ¹⁶ but Eli called him and said, "Samuel, my son."

Samuel answered, "Here I am."

¹⁷ "What was it he said to you?" Eli asked. "Do not hide it from me. May God deal with you, be it ever so severely, if you hide from me anything he told you." ¹⁸ So Samuel told him everything, hiding nothing from him. Then Eli said, "He is the Lord; let him do what is good in his eyes."

¹⁹ The Lord was with Samuel as he grew up, and he let none of Samuel's words fall to the ground. ²⁰ And all Israel from Dan to Beersheba recognized that Samuel was attested as a prophet of the Lord. ²¹ The Lord continued to appear at Shiloh, and there he revealed himself to Samuel through his word."

So much goodness in simply one chapter. Here was a boy who was a fulfillment of prayer for his mother, and he then was a fulfilled promised by his mother. He was now in the presence of the Lord and in the home of Eli, the prophet. This is where chapter 3 finds Samuel. As a mother myself, I try to image this experience for Samuel's mother, his family, and the house of Eli. The heritage of faithfulness is so profound, deep, rich, and generationally blessed. This is worth diving into but that is for another day.

For today we will step into the heart and mind of Samuel himself as chapter 3 unpacks this profound experience he has with the Lord.

We know Eli is a prophet and the presence of the Lord is upon him and his house. Samuel had been consecrated to the Lord from his birth, bringing him to Eli's home. The room in which Samuel was sleeping contained the Ark of God. Samuel was steeped in the knowledge of God, was witness to the presence of God, and was under the authority and wisdom of the prophet. Each day was filled with Godly teaching, knowledge, and fulfilled prophecy. His whole life was truly saturated in the presence of God. He was participating with all his teaching by ministering before the Lord under Eli.

So here was Samuel with proof upon proof of the heart of God, the truth of God, the fulfillment of God, and the knowledge of God. He was teaching about God and was ministering to others. And yet when God spoke to him, he did not recognize His voice.

[7] Now Samuel did not yet know the Lord: The word of the Lord had not yet been revealed to him.

Ok, hold up…how did he not recognize God's voice? How did he not know the Lord? Was he not paying attention to the teachings he had received? Was he somehow not ministering correctly? Had he not learned all the ways that God had showed Himself to His people? Had he not been doing everything he was supposed to do? Was he not living on every word Eli ever spoke to him?

Ah beloved, did you hear it? He was living on every word that his loving Eli had ever spoken, and truthfully, he should have perceived Eli's voice at this point in his story. Eli was faithful to his calling in raising Samuel up in the full knowledge of the Lord. Eli was entrusted with him, and as a prophet, the presence of the Lord was upon him. Samuel was paying attention to all the experiences he had ever witnessed and heard about. He was so faithful to the teachings he was under that when he heard the voice of the Lord he thought Eli was calling. He had learned to trust Eli completely and was fully obedient to him. Samuel had knowledge, he had witnessed amazing things, he loved Eli and was faithful to all the doings of his daily chores and teachings. Of course, Samuel should have trusted Eli's voice, *HAD* he called.

How easy is this for us? We give our lives to the Lord, we are consecrated to Him, we have knowledge and teachings that we can pass on to others, we minister from those truths, we can be faithful to the "doings" of our good knowledge, we can serve in the presence of the Lord, surrounded by anointed people, and yet we can miss when God calls our name. The knowledge of the Lord and knowledge of the presence of the Lord was not enough for Samuel to recognize God's voice and knowledge will not be enough for us either.

At this point, let's pause for a minute. We can see a deep pattern of knowledge here. Samuel was a prophet's student, an obedient son, a faithful follower, a seeker of good, and an external witness of God's presence. From all human accounts he would have been a "believer"; a follower of God, a student of the word, a good person, a knowledgeable teacher. He would have had influence as a student of the prophet, he would have had an audience for any knowledge he would be sharing, and he may have felt a sense of security in this. Perhaps he was learning to identify himself with his knowledge. Perhaps his foundations of legitimacy were grounded in knowledge and as a student of the prophet. Perhaps…

With all the knowledge that Samuel had, it was still not what he needed to recognize God's voice. Being in witness to the presence of God on others was not enough for him to personally recognize God's voice call his name. Being under teaching was not the equipping he needed to have the spirit to hear. All of his exposure, his knowledge, witnessing, hearing prophecy, and being externally surrounded by the presence of God was not the fulfillment of a personal relationship of intimacy in order to know God's voice. Samuel's experience with the Lord up until this point was knowledge and witness-based. It says that the word of the Lord had not come to him yet. At this point, the legitimacy of his relationship with the Lord was based on what had already been done, what he already knew, and who he knew to hold truth about God.

Here's good news. All of this is true and worth celebrating with Samuel. All of this was Samuel's experience, his upbringing, his training. His focus on learning, his witnessing, and his walk of obedience to his prophet prepare him for what happens next. All of this doesn't discount or lessen the rest of this amazing story – it actually allows for the fulfillment of the amazing prophet named Samuel. Praise the Lord. If you, beloved, find yourself in this portion of Samuel's reality, then hold on to your seat…God is about to do a new thing.

---

[8] A third time the Lord called, "Samuel." And Samuel got up and went to Eli and said, "Here I am; you called me."

Then Eli realized that the Lord was calling the boy. [9] So Eli told Samuel, "Go and lie down, and if he calls you, say, 'Speak, Lord, for your servant is listening.'" So Samuel went and lay down in his place.

[10] The Lord came and stood there, calling as at the other times, "Samuel. Samuel." Then Samuel said, "Speak, for your servant is listening."

True to the presence of the Lord on Eli, Eli had recognized that the Lord must be calling Samuel. We can give Eli a lot of grace here. He was not well; the Lamp of the Lord had not gone out on him yet, but it was dimming. He was an old man, sleeping and being awoken by his young prodigy in the middle of the night. I picture him groggy and slightly confused the first few times Samuel came to him. On the third time after being awoken, he then recognized what this must be. He knew now that God was calling on Samuel and he directed him as to what to say. True to Samuel's obedient heart, Samuel then did what Eli directed.

Picture this amazing scene: this young man who was so saturated in teachings from the teacher of all teachers of his time, Eli, the prophet. Samuel had an upbringing that included the presence of the Lord. This was unique for this time in God's story. As the Scripture says, "In those days the word of the Lord was rare; there were not many visions." God chose His presence to be upon Eli's house, and Samuel slept in the same room as the Ark of God. Now as the account continues, "The Lord came and stood there, calling as at the other times, Samuel, Samuel." Can you see this amazing scene? *God Stood There...* Samuel's now-personal God came and stood there and called Samuel's name. This young man, who up until this point had only known about God, now had God standing in his room.

When Eli told Samuel to respond to the call of God's voice, this is when Samuel was able to hear and see God. It took his beloved teacher to teach him the lesson of all lessons, how to say "yes." How to trust the call as the voice of God himself and out of faith say, "Speak, your servant is listening." It took Samuel taking a heart posture of being God's servant and agreeing to listen with not only his ears, but also his heart, soul, mind, and strength. It took Holy courage to forgo his personal processing of all he already knew about God, and Holy surrender to trusting this experience with the Lord in a completely new way. Samuel could have settled for knowledge and service, missing his birthright. What would have happened if Samuel refused to listen with his heart and soul? What if he refused to see something new and put all his faith in what already had been done? What if he simply refused to accept that this was God calling? What if he was fearful and chose to sleep through his personalized visit from God himself? The what-ifs can go on and on...but the outcome would have been a completely different story and the generational effects would have been astronomical. Samuel's birthright, his inheritance, the fulfillment of the call on him was dependant on this moment. This "yes" allowed for Samuel and God's personal, intimate relationship to begin. Samuel's "Speak, your servant is listening," was the colliding of knowledge and intimacy, making it possible for him to become one of the greatest prophets.

Samuel was entrusted with knowledge and service. Only when he surrendered to the presence of God, did the fullness of God's call on his life come to pass. "Love the Lord your God, with all your heart, mind, soul, and strength." When Samuel did, the fulfillment, the anointing fell fully on him, and the rest of his life was grounded in the personal, intimate presence of God.

From that moment forward, "The Lord was with Samuel as he grew up, and He let none of his words fall to the ground." Samuel was entrusted with speaking new things in God's story; life-changing teachings, anointing, equipping, and prophecies. "All of Israel recognized that Samuel was attested as a prophet of the Lord."

The focus for Samuel and the Lord became intimacy, worship, trust, fulfillment, and holy power. Notice with me that the fulfillment of knowledge and doctrine was found in worship, surrender, and intimacy. Celebrating and trusting the Lord first, made the way to hear His voice, His direction, His messages, His calling, His commissioning, and the fulfillment of grace, mercies, and empowerment. First Samuel was entrusted with vast knowledge; life-giving knowledge, and then he was called by name into intimate relationship with the Lord.

"Samuel? Samuel?"

"Speak, your servant is listening."

In Christ we hear God call our names, when we say yes, the presence of the Lord infills us with His Holy Spirit. Praise the Lord...From that day forward, He continues to stand by the "bed of our heart" and call our names, to procure more of our selves by His love, mercies, and endless grace. To move our relationship with Him into greater intimacy, to give us clear vision of who we are to Him. To speak words of calling and destiny over our lives. To give wisdom, discernment, and spiritual empowerment. God didn't discount Samuel's knowledge, He fulfilled it through intimacy with him, anointing Samuel with the full inheritance that was his to receive.

Position your heart today, beloved. God is calling your sweet name.

Thank you, Lord, for your gift of intellect, for being able to validate your truths with knowledge. Thank you for calling me to "know" about you and to know you through your word, your people, your anointed, and your wonders. Thank you that you don't leave me there. Draw me to receive the fullness of your inheritance.

In all authority of Jesus, I press back all barrier between you and me today, Lord. I ask you to cultivate the ground in my spirit to listen; to not only know you but to deeply know you. I ask for your holy confidence to hear you call my name and to say, "Speak Lord, your servant is listening." Draw me into deeper intimacy with you, Lord. My heart, mind, soul, and strength celebrate your power and your presence. Reveal your heart for me fully. I claim my legitimacy in my identity and relationship with you, Lord. Give me eyes to see you everywhere and see what you are doing. Never stop wooing me to a richness with you that leaves me in pure awe.

I love you, Lord. In Jesus's powerful name, amen.

References;
NIV Bible
Commentary from Charles R. Wale Jr.'s voice recording on the teacher; Arthur Burk

Day 4

Legacy of Promise

Oh beloved, I am excited for the beautiful layers and layers of goodness the Lord has for us. I picture a comfy chair, the softest blanket, a warm cup of steaming comfort, a quieting heart, and an invited Holy Spirit to cuddle up with you. Blessing, my friend.

We have all seen pictures, watched a documentary, or have seen in a movie where a desert was the land of choice. There are many details of the topography, the atmosphere, the eco-systems, and realities of the desert that make it distinct from all other regions on the planet. Here are only a few of those differences: Significant temperature fluctuations between day and night; it is dry, dusty, and the sand is an eroding agent. There is little ground water and vegetation is not comforting to the human condition. It is vast in size with undeniable impact on life dwelling there. A desert can be harsh in nature, dry in human provision, and a place of interdependency. At first glance, the desert is a place to avoid without planning and provision. It can drum up feelings of deep thirst, excess heat without shelter, a hopelessness of losing the way, and a sense of wandering aimlessly. Movies have capitalized on these truths, but for today I propose we take a deeper look at the value of the desert. Let's discover deep spaces of beauty, intimacy, and equipping in the desert; more than any other landscapes within the journey of faith, growth, and deeply knowing the God of the universe and lover of our souls.

"Ask and it will be given to you; seek and you will find; knock and the door will be opened to you. For everyone who asks receives; he who seeks finds and to him who knocks, the door will be opened" (Matthew 7:7-8).

Lord, we are here seeking, knocking, and asking for your presence. Reveal your heart for us and we ask the Holy Spirit to personalize this message for each of us this day. Lord, intersect us right where we are, and draw us into the deeper spaces of your fullness. We ask in Jesus's name, amen.

In the book of Acts, the stories of faith and action are amazing. I often have to remind myself that this is an account of live events; of real people, situations, and circumstances. They can seem so dramatic, exaggerated, and at times unreal. I intentionally notice that it's the same God, the same saving grace of Jesus, with the same Holy Spirit, serving His people in ways that bring awe, worship, wonder, and mystery.

Throughout Scripture we see real people being extraordinary people for the Kingdom. Today I want to settle in on one of them particularly; Paul. Here was a man who had an incredible gift to gather people, to mobilize people, to speak to the masses, and to follow through on the vision with world-changing commitment. When we first meet Paul, he still has the name Saul. He is a man on a mission to destroy or jail everyone who is proclaiming and believing the message of Jesus Christ and His salvation; everyone believing in The Way. Saul is a man of control and destruction. He has been given authority and has mobilized an army to follow him into the land to torture, kill, torment, or incarcerate all believers.

Picture the terror people must have felt when they heard and then saw the large, organized mob coming to their town, village, or home. Saul moved without remorse; he gave and followed direction with precision. He was so deeply entrenched in this mission that all opposition didn't even serve as a distraction. Saul was clearly self/mission-focused – nothing slowed him down. He didn't take a day off and he spent his time surrounded by people who supported his convictions.

Then as Saul was travelling to Damascus…

Saul's Conversion

[1]Meanwhile, Saul was still breathing out murderous threats against the Lord's disciples. He went to the high priest [2] and asked him for letters to the synagogues in Damascus, so that if he found any there who belonged

to the Way, whether men or women, he might take them as prisoners to Jerusalem. ³ As he neared Damascus on his journey, suddenly a light from Heaven flashed around him. ⁴ He fell to the ground and heard a voice say to him, "Saul, Saul, why do you persecute me?"

⁵ "Who are you, Lord?" Saul asked.

"I am Jesus, whom you are persecuting," He replied. ⁶ "Now get up and go into the city, and you will be told what you must do."

⁷ The men traveling with Saul stood there speechless; they heard the sound but did not see anyone. ⁸ Saul got up from the ground, but when he opened his eyes he could see nothing. So they led him by the hand into Damascus. ⁹ For three days he was blind, and did not eat or drink anything. ¹⁰ In Damascus there was a disciple named Ananias. The Lord called to him in a vision, "Ananias."

"Yes, Lord," he answered.

¹¹ The Lord told him, "Go to the house of Judas on Straight Street and ask for a man from Tarsus named Saul, for he is praying. ¹² In a vision he has seen a man named Ananias come and place his hands on him to restore his sight."

The account is simplistic in word but the details are world changing. Imagine with me a road of that time, a long walk ahead of them, deep detestation in his heart with papers in his pocket to prove it, an anxious pace as the mission lay ahead, conversations steeped with resolve to vicious doings, and profound internal unrest. This is what "a sudden light from Heaven" interrupted. Even with all the footing of resolve under Saul's feet, when the light came, Saul fell to the ground. Saul knew this was Divine presence because he asked, "Who are you, Lord?" (*love how he calls him Lord. Even without knowledge Saul *knew* this was the Lord). Jesus continued to tell Saul who He was and what he was to do next. Short and sweet, to the point and without further question. I can imagine the looks on Saul's travelling henchmen as they heard all of this – astounded.

This is truly extraordinary. Verses 8 and 9 are profound and begin the journey Saul has in becoming the Apostle Paul. When Saul got up from the ground he could see nothing; he had been blinded. Speechless from what they'd just heard and true to Saul's gift of mobilizing people, his henchmen took him to Damascus, leading him by the hand.

Here is the moment that changed every moment before it and in front of it. The Lord intersected Saul's life in the middle of his own personal agenda. Jesus introduced himself to Saul. Saul surrendered all and entered into relationship with the Lord. This self-driven man was about to make history again.

---

⁹ For three days he was blind, and did not eat or drink anything.

The significance of these three days strikes me profoundly. Saul was a man on a mission. He had incredible gifts of gathering a following, powerful support, and a ruthless army, which was backed by political and religious leaders. He was a man who never took a minute's rest to consider options; a man with influence, power, and authority to cast forth and to follow through. Now here he was, having encountered the living God and the first thing Jesus did was create circumstances for Saul to have undivided time and attention with the Lord. For three days Saul prayed and fasted. Saul needed a new heart, mind, soul and strength that was saturated with the Holy Spirit, and time alone with Him was the only way to get it. Jesus forced Saul into this place of darkness, newness, hunger, thirst, complete dependency, and need. Saul faced the reality of complete life-work change, uprooting all he knew, believed in, and stood for. Saul had a three-day desert experience; external dryness, physical depletion, and spiritual erosion with vast sands of truth. There was no release from the transforming heat and coolness of the new life being forged within him. For three days he was in the Lord's presence, receiving an impartation of the Lord. For three days he participated with transforming healing and knowledge of who the living God, Jesus is. Without interruption Saul was seeking and was receiving power, and he would leave that three days never being the same. Saul's heart emerged with more transformation and deeper resolve than ever before. Jesus had transformed this world changer into a world changer for the Kingdom.

Saul's sight was returned to him, and with new vision he began his public ministry. His ability to gather people, to mobilize people, to cast a larger audience, to enter relationship with a vast variety of people were now for the purposes of the Gospel and not for self-righteousness. Saul became the Apostle Paul. Those three days of transformation made way for a powerful ministry of person to person, village to village, city to city, and land to land. The beginning of his ministry proved impact was for the person, the immediate audience, and the generation he was in. He ushered-in the Gospel everywhere he went, and shook the dust off his clothes as he left areas where people did not listen. He was a man on immediate mission.

As Paul's ministry-scope increased, so did the opposition. He was made to be a world-changing doer. This amazing mission Paul was called to included busyness of travel, preaching, calling forth, gathering, and so much more. He followed the Lord's direction with precision. When God said go, he went. When He said stay, he stayed. After all Paul's journeying, his true focus was the heart of God, the saving grace of Jesus, and the power of the Holy Spirit. Paul lived his life from intentional intimacy with the Lord.

Paul was completely under the authority of Christ and nothing came to him without passing through God's approval first. That sounds so harsh. Paul was persecuted with great force, was rejected by so many people, and had horrible physical conditions and circumstances. Story after story tells of times that included forced isolation; years and years of prison; cold, hard floors and walls; hunger; thirst; filth; freezing and excessive heat; and eroding sands of time and flesh, which all added to the vast assault of the senses. It was a time of no rights; no external voice; no worldly comforts; no excessive movement; no vast immediate impact; and no power to change it. The sheer number of times this man was beaten, abandoned, shunned, tortured, hungry, thirsty, isolated, and rejected would be enough for anyone to waver in faith, and yet Paul never lost sight of the truth he was to share. This is truly an amazing truth about Paul's gifting and anointing. There was desert time after desert time in Paul's ministry, and he chose Christ each time. Paul didn't spend his time in discouragement, in fear of man, in pleasing people, in self-pity, or in victimization. He wasn't distracted by the circumstances he was in. He didn't dismiss the opportunity of intimacy with his Father. This is a mind-blowing truth about Paul that is unprecedented. God created times in Paul's life that were by world standards, dry lands, extreme desert places, great oppression, and without fruit. Paul's first desert was three days in length, equipping him for his immediate mission. This was followed by extreme desert places where the Holy Spirit cultivated and activated the authority and message for endless generations to come. These desert after deserts would have been harsh if not brutal. It was time apart that from human eyes would have been devastating, but from Kingdom perspective these experiences changed history. This is where God turned the world standard on its head.

Oh beloved of the Living God, let's look at the desert as the Lord sees it. This desert was used to deepen the intimacy between Paul and his God. This time was a time of hearing, seeing, and deeply knowing the God who saves. The Lord didn't allow all of this to conditionally punish Paul – no it was in these times the God of the universe could have Paul all to himself. Paul the goer, doer, and world changer had to have time set apart with the Lord. Intimacy with the God who speaks depended on it. These isolating deserts were needed for God to have the undivided attention of his audience of one. Paul lived through horrendous circumstances and was used by God to write vast amounts of New Testament Scripture for the greatest book in history, over all time, and for all time. He sat in those horrible prisons for years on end and wrote the living word that breathes to this very day.

Oh beloved, our human eyes can see the pain and suffering of desert times, but when we look at the desert through God's eyes we can see beauty beyond description. Intimacy with our God will require time set apart perhaps even in dry, eroding, deserts to seek His face, His voice, His comfort, His heart, and His power.

Desert lands forge spaces within us for the Lord to reign in His fullness. Time apart cultivates purpose and mission in the going and doing. Seeking His fullness brings wisdom to the eroding sands, freedom to the captives, light to the darkness, and living water to the desert. Intimacy with our loving Father actualizes the anointing on His children, equipping, empowering, and loving us fully to be the world changers the Lord chooses each one of us to be.

Oh beloved, see God's heart in the desert… Generations may depend on it.

Lord I come to you with a deep need to exhale. I can get so busy going and doing things in your name, or in my own, that I miss the times set apart by you. Lord increase my sensitivity to your voice as you invite me to draw away with you. Today I choose to follow you into those sacred yet difficult places. Speak Lord, you have my attention.

Where you draw me into the desert I proclaim you as all I will ever need. Grow me up to the fullness of the inheritance you have for me here. Speak deep into my spirit the message of your living salvation. Transfigure my heart, mind, soul, and strength to be the world changer you created me to be. I lay down expectations of what that might mean and fully trust you are so far ahead of me. I choose you Jesus, I choose your presence, I choose your equipping and mission. Where I step my foot, may your Kingdom come. Praise you for interrupting my own agenda and aligning me with yours. In Jesus's saving name, amen.

---

*References;
NIV Bible
Commentary from Charles R. Wale Jr.'s voice recording on the exhorter; Arthur Burk

Day 5

How Far Lord?

I love the Lord and His heart for each one of us. Thank you for joining me today, beloved. Get comfy, settle in, and prepare your heart to receive more of His heart for you. He keeps revealing more and more and more. Don't you just love that about Him?

I love reading about Jesus's miracles. It is simply astonishing to my human mind to put myself there; to see the scene from the perspective of one of the many. I catch myself before I mentally categorize it as one of His miracles. This doesn't make it any less miraculous, but it does pose the risk of us thinking it to be something to witness while not seeing some of the deeper, personalized messages for each one of us today.

Today let's take a look at one of Jesus's miracles and discover together what is available for us.

Lord, you are a miraculous God and you have us in awe of who you are. Lord, we ask you today to personalize your miracle to each of our hearts, minds, souls, and strengths. Thank you, Lord that you are that God. We love you. In Jesus's powerful name, amen.

Jesus Feeds the Five Thousand

John 6 ⁵ When Jesus looked up and saw a great crowd coming toward him, he said to Philip, "Where shall we buy bread for these people to eat?" ⁶ He asked this only to test him, for he already had in mind what he was going to do.

⁷ Philip answered him, "It would take more than half a year's wages to buy enough bread for each one to have a bite."

⁸ Another of his disciples, Andrew, Simon Peter's brother, spoke up, ⁹ "Here is a boy with five small barley loaves and two small fish, but how far will they go among so many?"

¹⁰ Jesus said, "Have the people sit down." There was plenty of grass in that place, and they sat down (about five thousand men were there). ¹¹ Jesus then took the loaves, gave thanks, and distributed to those who were seated as much as they wanted. He did the same with the fish.

¹² When they had all had enough to eat, he said to his disciples, "Gather the pieces that are left over. Let nothing be wasted." ¹³ So they gathered them and filled twelve baskets with the pieces of the five barley loaves left over by those who had eaten.

I was twenty-three when I surrendered my life to Jesus. I fall short to describe my gratitude or to share the depth of a twenty plus-year relationship that is forever growing. Over these years I have read this passage many times. It never disappoints to cast a vision of a hillside covered in people, in a period of time that is far from my own. I imagine their clothing, their beards, their sandals covered in dust, and the looks of anticipation on each face as they listen to Jesus speak. They walked miles to hear Him. Whether it was curiosity or spiritual hunger that brought them, none the less they took a leap of faith and showed up. A great crowd, a huge crowd, gathering together. What they didn't take into account was how long they would be there. As the passage says, they didn't have means to feed themselves. The men didn't pack a meal, an extra snack, or a little midnight lunch. In the other Gospels it says the disciples were asking Jesus to dismiss them so they could go buy their own food. I suppose it could be likened to a mega conference or gathering in today's world, except no indoor facility, no chairs, no air conditioning and certainly no concessions, food trucks, or caterers on site prepared to feed the masses their supper. These people simply followed Jesus out to the countryside to hear Him speak.

In true Jesus fashion He already had a solution to the food shortage. He knew ahead of time how long they would be there, He knew how many people would be there, and nothing was a surprise or coincidence. He was fully ahead of their "knowing." As pointed out in Matthew referring to the 5000 men actually meant men had also brought their families. So it was 5000 men plus their wives and children. We can only estimate how many thousands of people were truly there, but the fact that there were thousands and thousands is mind bending.

Love how in verse 5 Jesus asks Philip where they can buy bread for everyone, just to test Philip, for Jesus already had in mind what He was going to do. Giving the response that would be completely understandable to give; [7] Philip answered him, "It would take more than half a year's wages to buy enough bread for each one to have a bite."

Philip and the other disciples were being practical, logical, and sensible. Over half a year's wages and being miles from town made buying bread for a single bite for everyone seem hardly worth it. A verse down, Andrew speaks up and says, "Here is a boy with five small barley loaves and two small fish, but how far will they go among so many?" Honestly, if we didn't know what Jesus was about to do next would we not ask the same question? "But how far will this small amount go among so many?"

I am loving the journey of revelation with you, beloved. May the familiar take on a whole new vision as we continue.

There is one person in this story who is so easy to overlook. It's a person who has the heart of a giver and takes one of the greatest risks in this whole account…the boy.

Join me as we see him sitting with his family. In this sea of bodies; men, women, and children, was this boy. Culturally, children were more seen than heard. Whatever the child did was a reflection on his family's honour and reputation. The man would speak for his family and held the responsibility of social order. Even the passages written don't mention wives and children, who simply didn't carry the same social value as men did. So from these general pieces of information we can deduct that a child going forward with a gift was a great risk.

I try to imagine how this may have taken place. Did the boy have his parents' blessing to go forward and if he did why didn't his dad do it, for that would have been proper. Perhaps the boy didn't have his parents' permission but knew he had to go. If that was the case, there was a huge spiritual, physical, social, economic, and personal risk in stepping out in faithful obedience. That risk would have included personal consequences for stepping away from established social dynamics. And what about the economic impact five loaves and two fish had on his family financially? Was he taking food out of his family's mouths in order to give these items away? Was he making the choice between possible family hunger to give a gift that didn't make sense in regards to the true need of this massive crowd? Perhaps families around him were urging him to share this portion with them. It would have meant feeding five families and there would have been a lot of praise, making it possible to feed his own ego, for making such a personal sacrifice to feed so many. Perhaps he was sitting far off and had to commit to getting these loaves and fish up to the disciples, weaving in and out of people for a long distance. Regardless of all the possible circumstances around how this boy brought these five barley loaves and two fish to the disciples, they pale beside the fact that he did. Foregoing his security, his ego, his family order and commitments, his social positioning, financial considerations, and physical hunger, he brought forward a sacrificial gift.

The innocence of a child is so genuine. He would have been there with hands wide open giving these loaves and fish with an authentic heart of giving. No strings attached, no conditions on how to use the food, and no expectation of receiving it back in full. It was truly a surrendered offering. The heart of a giver was within this boy. He saw a massive need; a need he had no way of making any real difference in, but he knew who could. He knew he could bring this provision to Jesus and somehow it would be enough. After all it was all he had to offer.

The Lord tells us in Scripture to come unto Him like little children, with this beautiful innocence of trust, faith, and a deeper hope of possibility. Just like the boy bringing all that he had, logically knowing it wasn't enough to make a significant impact and coming any way presenting his portion with faith that didn't need to know the outcome before the offering was given. There is an innocence in presentation, of surrender, of childlike faith exemplified for us here.

We are to come with the provisions, the gifts, talents, abilities, and dreams that we have been given taking similar risks of forgoing social norms, financial implications, surrendering personal gains, and the outcome to bring forward our five loaves and two fish. We all have a portion within us and it is easy to justify that it won't make a difference to the mass need of the world around us. To disqualify ourselves based on our age, social positioning, economics, geographic location, and the great crowd of the more qualified. Just like this boy, we too know our offering won't make a big difference on its own but we know within whose hands that it could.

The passage then continues with Jesus receiving this boy's offering. Jesus broke it, blessed it, distributed it, and it multiplied exponentially. This small gift fed 5000 men, their wives, and children until everyone was full. Then to top it off they gathered the leftovers, as to waste nothing, and they filled twelve baskets. Nothing is too small, disqualified, or ineligible for Jesus to bless for his Gospel purposes.

It says in verse 6 that Jesus already had in mind what he was going to do. He knew this boy was going to give all he had, which at first appearance was too small to make significant difference. Jesus knew it was all He needed to exemplify this generational blessing. This mere five loaves and two fish was enough to feed the immediate generations of people on that hillside, and it was also enough to make generation after generation's impact for the Gospel.

That boy and his family had no idea of the impact their offering would have. What they did know was they needed to get it into the hands of Jesus, knowing He in His goodness and Godness would take this small offering and do exponentially more than they could ask or imagine.

It took taking their faith and putting it into action, which looked like a huge risk, in order to see the fulfillment of Jesus in verse 5, "for He already had in mind what He was going to do."

Beloved, where are your five loaves and two fish? With childlike faith, bring them to Jesus, forgo all the messages of the world around you and the dialogue within you, putting your faith into action, presenting your offering with open hands and surrendered heart and risking all that this is by simply putting it into Jesus's hands.

He wants to receive it from you, knowing full well He already has in mind what He is going to do with it. Allow Him to break it open and bless it, and He may very well feed generations with the provision He has entrusted to you. He wastes nothing. Nothing too small, disqualified or ineligible for Jesus's Kingdom purposes. Take the risk, stand up, forgo the expectations around you, weave through the masses, and with childlike faith present your five loaves and two fish to the one who can multiply it exponentially. He has plans, beloved, He has plans.

Lord, thank you for showing me your heart through a little boy. Give me your Kingdom eyes to see my gifts the way you do. To see the gifts you have given me, not so I can have glory, but to bring them back to you with trust, faith, and beautiful risk, knowing you already have in mind what you will do with them. Lord, I ask your Holy Spirit to seal the prompting you just set in my heart. With Holy courage I present to you my mere five loaves and two fish with no expectations but with great anticipation of your goodness. You are a God of miracles and with child-like faith I position my heart for the miracle you are about to do. Lord, take this small offering and multiply it for your Gospel purposes. In Jesus's miraculous name, amen.

References;
NIV Bible
Commentary from Charles R. Wale Jr.'s voice recording on the giver;
Arthur Burk

Day 6

Redemption Power

The word of God is such a gift to each one of us. There's so much life on see-through paper painted with his voice of love.

Jesus said in John, "If you hold to my teaching, you are really my disciples. Then you will know the truth and the truth will set you free."

Let's explore together today a portion of our birthright and our inheritance as children of the God on high. Beloved, set apart time, gather your favorite prayer closet accessories, and join me on a journey of obedience to freedom.

Lord, we ask for your presence today. We ask for your revelation of truth, knowing that revelation is only the beginning. Solidify your truth in our hearts, minds, souls, and strength on this day, for today we seek your promised freedom. In Jesus's freeing name, amen.

Let's go back to the beginning…In the garden on the sixth day there were two things that happened, which I think hold a freedom key for us. First, this is the day that man was created, God breathed His very breath into Adam, and therefore the human spirit was birthed. The intimacy between God's Spirit and ours began with that first breath. Our very breath is His breath, breath of true life. The second thing that happened was God spoke a blessing over His crowning creation and a commissioning of purpose. "Be fruitful and increase in number; fill the earth and subdue it. Rule over the fish of the sea and the birds of the air and over every living creature that moves on the ground" (Gen 1:28). God designed man and woman to be fruitful and live in stewardship of dominion over creation.

Why is this important in regards to today, to our own personal freedom in Christ, our identity and design? The heartbeat of our loving Father is saturated in these verses. First; His heart for His crowning creation, you and me, is so valuable to Him that nothing less than His all-encompassing breath would do. Picture God leaning over Adam's lifeless body, and with a moment beyond description, his breath entering Adam's lungs. Adam's heart starts beating, blood starts flowing, and life within Him begins. He opens his eyes to look directly into God's. I picture the smile on God's face as He slowly leans back to allow Adam to rise, knowing full well the choices man will make, the years it will take for redemption and the thousands of years before this will all come full circle. Still, nothing less than God's own living breath would do. The human spirit and life was born.

To add to this, God gave a great call to his crowning creation. He entrusted Adam and Eve with all He had created on the first six days. They were called to steward, to resource well, to manage, to create systems, to expand, and to move in the freedom of spiritual authority. This commissioning was given in the untainted garden, was given to the sin-free couple, and was entrusted as part of God's holiness. This is so important to note, as God has beautiful, holy purposes for rule and dominion. It was after the design of His holy purposes that sin entered the world and the perversion in understanding this commissioning also began.

Today's English uses the words "rule" or "dominion" to mean control, overpower, and negatively dominate. God's heart is so different from our merely sinful nature and English definitions. He called Adam and Eve to have dominion over all other creation, not to dominate God's crowning creation, other people, or to use creation for self-serving purposes. They were called forth to populate the earth, not to abuse it for their need for control. From the fall of man we have misunderstood God's heart and His commissioning in the garden.

Sin not only set in motion the wrong version of this commissioning, but it also includes the cost of this misconception.

We each feel the cost of sin every day. We feel deep in our spirits the discontentedness of this world that is not our home even if our lives are abundant by worldly standards. We each have within us that desire for God to walk and talk with us in the garden; never being outside of His intimate presence. Since the beginning we are designed for that intimacy and commissioning. After all, beloved, we are His crown creation.

As we live in a fallen world with a spirit desirous of garden intimacy and purposes, we have a choice as to what will rule our hearts, minds, souls, and strengths.

We each know that in Christ we can do all things, that we are more than conquerors, that we have new life and in Christ we have freedom. I am wondering if you are like me in that this is not always my reality. There are times when my bondage is comfortable and predictable, and therefore I participate in it without even knowing I just chose it or even worse, knowing full well what it is and choosing it anyway. Also there are times where I feel far from strong or able to conquer anything, letting my sight lead me versus faith. There are times when I can be paralyzed by fear, the unknown, or even success, being frozen to the spiritual ground I am standing on and not able to move to the narrow path set before me. There are also times where I find myself not wanting to stay on the narrow path because my flesh, soul, mind, or desire perceives the wide path as less work, more fun, socially acceptable, and simply easier in every way. There are times when the slavery of Egypt calls my name, where my memories deceive me into thinking that at least I had food in Egypt. I know each participation brings me to the place of deep heaviness, distress, sadness, oppression, and a sense of dying inside. The spirit of slavery tries hard to regain ground in my life by making the world around me look more comfortable or by whispering false identity and making it sound normal to me.

I am grateful that the Lord is not offended by me. That He knows each piece of me and with loving kindness He whispers His heart to mine. He restores my footing as

His beloved daughter. Oh how I praise Him for loving me so profoundly.

He made you and me, He knows how many hairs are on each of our heads, and He has been with us from day one, so nothing about us shocks Him. He is kind and patient. He is for us. In His kindness and patience He also doesn't leave us in our slavery without a way out.

Romans 8:12-17

[12] So, my brothers and sisters, you owe the flesh nothing. You do not need to live according to its ways, so abandon its oppressive regime. [13] For if your life is just about satisfying the impulses of your sinful nature, then prepare to die. But if you have invited the Spirit to destroy these selfish desires, you will experience life. [14] If the Spirit of God is leading you, then take comfort in knowing you are His children. [15] You see, you have not received a spirit that returns you to slavery, so you have nothing to fear. The Spirit you have received adopts you and welcomes you into God's own family. That's why we call out to Him, "Abba, Father," as we would address a loving daddy.

[16] Through that prayer, God's Spirit confirms in our spirits that we are His children. [17] If we are God's children, that means we are His heirs along with the Anointed, set to inherit everything that is His. If we share His sufferings, we know that we will ultimately share in His glory.

Romans 8 is a treasure trove of pure goodness. Identity securing, foundation building, authority giving, and life-breathing truth; verse after verse of freedom.

This process from moving from slavery into freedom in Christ is a journey. It entails putting one foot in front of the other on a bridge of obedience. It does our hearts good to look back to see how far the Lord has brought us. Spending this time of recollection in rejoicing, with gratitude, with praise for all He has done, brought us up and out of and brought us into. Also this give us the holy courage needed to be intentional, facing giants, big or small, to keep walking and obeying. Each one of these steps takes us farther and farther away from Egypt and from the pull of slavery.

Let's look at slavery. This word instantly brings a very clear picture to our minds. We see how slavery looks in the world around us, throughout history as well as within ourselves. It is an emotional picture, it is a graphic picture in our minds, and strong beliefs rise up within us of how we view slavery. This word casts a clear image and definition.

What I do want to look at for a moment is the rights of a slave. Do they have any? Do slaves have opinions, voices, and the ability to be themselves? Does a slave have a choice or freedoms? We know with heartbreaking certainty that a slave has no immediate rights, no choice, no freedom, and no humanization. They are a commodity, a resource, and replaceable. Even just writing all these realities brings tears as we know the extreme cost of slavery to God's crowning creation. As we think about this in the physical, our very souls cry out for justice, for freedom, and for redemption. We feel ourselves rising up to give a voice to the oppressed, to step into the gap to break chains, to fight for those without defense, and to set a path for many more to do the same. Everything about us is moved to deep disdain at the realities of slavery physically, emotionally, mentally, and spiritually.

In contrast let's look at what it means to be a son or daughter of the Most-High King. What are the rights of His children? Do His children have opinions, voices and the ability to be themselves? Does His child have applicable choice and freedoms? Does His daughter/son have a loving father, a provider, a protector, a consoler, a friend, a place at the family table, a knee to cuddle up on, a spoken blessing, and a generational inheritance? Yes; a resounding yes. Scripture states again and again the freedoms a child of God possesses; the birthright, privilege, anointing, salvation, inheritance, and above all, choice. As beautifully outlined in

---

Romans 8:14-15, "If the Spirit of God is leading you, then take comfort in knowing you are His children. You see, you have not received a spirit that returns you to slavery, so you have nothing to fear. The Spirit you have received adopts you and welcomes you into God's own family. That's why we call out to Him, "Abba. Father!" as we would address a loving daddy."

We may be far from Eden and yet God's mercy is not finished. His heart of hearts is to move each one of us from slavery to the fullness we have as children of God Almighty.

From our birth, even if our childhoods were beautiful, we have had messages and realities that have spoken loudly against our identity as children of God; children with rights, voices, freedoms, and choice. These messages may be against us but the truth is, God was there first; His original design, His breath, His righteousness, His choice and anointed purposes for each one of us. He didn't loosely decide the details, the time in history, or the color of our eyes, No. Of all the wonders of the world, we are the ones that take His breath away.

We do not have control over many circumstances, sins against us, our original upbringing, identity spoken over us, our very DNA, and so much more but what we do have is the choice of how to respond. "So, my brothers and sisters, you owe the flesh nothing. You do not need to live according to its ways, so abandon its oppressive regime. For if your life is just about satisfying the impulses of your sinful nature, then prepare to die. But if you have invited the Spirit to destroy these selfish desires, you will experience life" (Verse 12-13). Beloved, we owe our flesh nothing, this includes old habits, thought patterns, beliefs, understanding, knowledge, experience, response patterns, and simply everything that is not life-giving to ourselves and those around us.

Another way the Lord says it is in 2 Corinthians 5:17, "Therefore, if anyone is in Christ, he is a new creation. The old has passed away; behold, the new has come." We are a new creation. Everything from our yesterdays has passed away, God has done a new thing in each one of us from the moment we surrendered to His loving invitation for salvation and relationship.

We may be products of our past, but we are not prisoners to it. "So if the son sets you free, you will be free indeed."

Beloved, this is where God's faithfulness pours out in a word…Choice. We are God's children, sons and daughters, therefore we have full privilege and right of choice.

As new creations, as children of the living God, we have the opportunity to choose life, to choose the living breath of our Abba father, to choose freedom. We have the choice to hear the commissioning of the sixth day of creation and step into God's heart and true meaning of ruling over all creation. Through closer examination of our lives, our hearts, minds, souls, and strengths we can find the sinful, wrong version of dominion and rule. Revelation through examination is the beginning of true transformation. Take some time here to look for those wrong versions of dominion and rule in your own heart, mind, soul, and strength. Where have we made agreements with wrong versions of thinking, believing, doing, and responding? Where do we feel and see the bondage or oppression of slavery? Are we experiencing and agreeing with any self-deprecating thinking, limiting beliefs, subdued souls, enchained emotions, grips of unforgiveness, or truly a multitude of other wrong versions of dominion and rule in our lives, hearts, minds, souls, and strength?

Beloved, bring each revelation to our loving Father with humble repentance leaving fear, the need for control, selfish ambitions, and slavery to domination at the feet of the only one who can restore us to His original design. Let us intentionally enter into the presence of our living God, letting Him breathe His living breath into our lungs once again, to look into our eyes and speak our belovedness to us. Embrace the birthright, the inheritance, and the first commissioning from the garden as an intimate child of God. You beloved, are His chosen.

Heavenly Father, thank you for the gift of your living breath. Lord, draw me up and into the fullness of your Holy calling, your commissioning from the very beginning. Bring revelation for any and all of the wrong versions of dominion I have participated in. Draw me into your presence, hear my heart of repentance. Cultivate your ruler-calling within us.

Empower me to steward, to resource well, to manage, to create systems, to expand, and to move in the freedom of spiritual authority in and over the world you have entrusted to me. Cast a clear vision in my mind of your design in power, not force. Lord, fill me with your spirit to overflowing – may I be the steward you called me to be. In your commissioning name, amen.

References;
NIV Bible
Commentary from Charles R. Wale Jr.'s voice recording on the ruler; Arthur Burk

Day 7

God has the Best Ideas

Oh beloved, I find myself rejoicing beyond words today as I anticipate this time with you. The Lord's goodness has been lavish and pure, far more than I could ask or imagine. I have gathered my favourite accessories to accompany me into the presence of the Most-High, join me with your favorites and let's journey in together.

Lord God, you are, you have always been and will forever be. We are but a breath in the context of eternity and yet you have chosen us to move mountains with faith the size of mustard seeds. Lord, meet us in our doings today and draw us into simply being with you. Quieten our hearts, minds, souls, and strengths to meet you in a fresh way. We ask this in your eternal name, amen.

"He says, Be Still and know that I am God; I will be exalted among the nations, I will be exalted in the earth. The Lord Almighty is with us; the God of Jacob is our fortress" (Psalm 46:10-11 NIV).

Love this verse on so many levels. It calls us into ceasing our doings, it beckons our heart to trust, and it draws our spirit higher in worship for our Almighty God. The high calling to Be and Know is only possible when we see the heart of the Most-High God and trust Him with simply everything. This verse can draw an exhale from the deepest parts of our souls.

The calling in this verse is to *be*, not to do. It is to know him, not intellectualize him. It is an opposite voice of that of the world around us. We live in a very busy, noisy world, making it easy to hear the common messages of *keep busy for the sake of being busy* as well as *striving is surviving; success is in accomplishment*. Not to mention the mental jungle gym we are constantly navigating and emotional dichotomies that can keep us exhausted. The sheer volume of noise, the good, the bad and the indifferent, is enough for each of us to pass over this verse with a hopelessness of the unachievable.

Oh beloved, great news. The voice of love calls us to the opposite. No achieving needed, no to-do list, no schedule to conquer, no striving. He says to simply come be, come know, exhale, enter in, and savour.

Jesus beckons us to come as Mary did. He calls us to sit at his feet and enjoy His presence, to hear His voice, to draw from His holiness, to pleasure in simplicity, to revel in awe, and to savour every moment. As the verse continues He shares some of the after-glows of His presence, which are rejoicing, praising, knowing truth among the nations, and professing that He is Almighty God. So much goodness birthed from His presence.

As easy as it would be to enter into the familiar discussion comparing Mary and Martha, the truth is Jesus loves the doer and the be'er. He loves every Mary and Martha moment we can have. He created Mary and Martha and the wonderful character within them. They are each a reflection of His image, fearfully and wonderfully made. No shame or condemnation. Simply a calling upon each of our hearts, regardless if we are more a doer or a be'er, to enter into times of quiet, deeply knowing, savouring presence. Taking a break from the busyness to get to know our God, His heart, and will, and to receive reconciliation, alignment, and truly a million other impartations.

Being still is not a passive state, although there is rest, entering in is an intentional posture. Once choosing to participate by entering into His presence, then our "work" is done. The rest is the waves upon waves of impartation of pure goodness from Almighty God.

"Here I am. I stand at the door and knock. If anyone hears my voice and opens the door, I will come in and eat with that person, and they with me" (Revelations 3:20 NIV).

Let's have a little fun. Recall a special family dinner. Take your time, and with every prompting notice the memory increase...What is the time of day, the time of year, the time in your history? Whose home is this in? Picture the table on which dinner was shared, notice the presence or absence of décor on the table, the number of chairs and how high or low-backed they are. Notice if it is a set table or set up buffet style. Thinking to the food now, was it prepared by one person or was it a family potluck? Are the food choices made from tradition or are they a common provision? See the serving bowls, the size of serving spoons, the steam rising from hot pots, the aroma of pure deliciousness filling the air. Is the kitchen buzzing with activity, people, and the delightful noise of laughter and directives, or is everyone seated while one beautiful soul serves the family with love? Notice now who is around your table. See their faces, notice their eyes, their smiles, and their hearts. How old is everyone there? Is there someone telling a great story or is everyone having individual conversations around the table? Who is the first to share an encouraging word or crack a joke? Is there a peaceful quietness or vast sound, both cultivating the wholeness of belonging? Notice how long everyone lingers around the table. How does the table get cleared? Is there an announcement of "time to clear," or does someone just begin? Is clean-up an organized humming of activities or an organized team of only a few?

Special family dinners are memories to be cherished, savoured, and revisited.

Oh beloved, notice how you feel at this moment as your memories allow you to relive the beauty of this family dinner. Every detail draws us deeper into the joy of savouring. Even now savouring the savouring is steeped in His goodness.

As wonderfully as our memories serve us, they are only a small reflection of the beautiful family dinner

Jesus promises here. "Here I am. I stand at the door and knock. If anyone hears my voice and opens the door, I will come in and eat with that person, and they with me" (Revelations 3:20).

Dinner with Jesus…what would we make to eat?

No need to cook, beloved; He promises to bring dinner, every time. The bread of life and living water that we may never hunger or thirst again. He invites us to open the door and He does the rest. He comes in, He brings dinner, and we get to simply savour. He brings the background music of true belonging and being known. He adorns the table with joy, laughter, and rich inheritance stories. He brings the centerpiece and place settings of intimacy, transparency, and authenticity. He brings bowl upon bowl of peace, holiness, sanctification, love, kindness, goodness, and so much more to feast on without limit or fear of excess. He looks us in the eyes and smiles from ear to ear with unhindered love. He belly laughs at our jokes and listens intently to our stories. He is in no hurry to leave the table and invites us to linger with Him longer, to hear every syllable spoken, noticing the nuances, depths in breath, the power of presence, embracing the wonder and the familiar, to talk, to listen, to share, to be, to know… He calls us to simply savour every detail of being in His presence and then to come and do it again tomorrow. In true abundance, He fills us to overflowing so that we have all of it to share with others.

This week, I asked the Lord to show me a glimpse of his heart on this matter. I was very intentional about finding moments in my daily life to savour where I was so in the moment that no thought distracted, no noise called me away, and nothing was more important than the moment I was in. I discovered a pureness that was only possible because of intention and being deliberate in participation letting the moments become about the soul and spirit with little to do with intellect.

The Lord showed me in one moment specifically, His heart for His beautiful children.

I have a now-adult son. It is an amazing reality that my child, who use to lay his head on my chest, is now 6'3 and the embrace has reversed. We are a huggy family and we hold embraces for a breath or two longer if we can, savouring the moment. In this particular moment as Steven hugged me goodbye before he left the house, I had my ear right over his heart. Once again, it stopped me in my tracks. There is such pureness in the heartbeat of one's child; such life-giving goodness with every beat. My mother heart exploded with expression beyond mere words. The fulfillment of love, the gift, the chosenness, the belonging, the heartbeat of my very soul was beating back to me through my ears as I listened. With every beat I savoured even deeper, not wanting to ever forget the fulfillment in this moment. The richness of the heartbeat of my beloved child speaks an unspoken message so deeply within me that I am a better person as I lift my ear from his chest. A moment of the richest savouring changed me again that day as it drew me back to remembering the fullness of this relationship. It is pure soul food, to simply be and know with deep intimacy the heart of my beloved.

This is a small expression of our heavenly Father's heart for us. He calls and draws us into His safe embrace to hear His heartbeat; again and again. To know the depths of who He is and who we are in Him, to have such intimacy, belonging, and liberty to simply be. To enter into His presence with full surrender to the moment. The world becomes quiet, the spirit melts into assurance, the release of expectation and agenda is evident, and the savouring is cultivated deep within the spirit. A stillness resides in the being, and a joy fills the space in the knowing. The pureness is beyond words and the heart of the Father is like no other. This intimacy is far beyond intellect, far beyond description as heartbeats speak a language without words. All of our knowing melts away to receive a deeper knowing of Father God.

"Be Still and Know that I am God. Here I am. I stand at the door and knock."... May our spirit hear the knocking...Answer it, beloved. You will see the greatest smile as His eyes meet yours, stepping in with a feast to share without condition. Enter the embrace of presence and listen deeply to the heartbeat of your loving Father. Let him adorn your heart, mind, soul, and strength with the most spectacular expressions of His holiness. His desire is to show you how He sees you, to bestow the fullness of what love really looks like, and to endow you with a richness of His character, His heart, His mind, His breath, and His nature. Notice that the blessing doesn't depend on you, it is who He is. He is Love. There is so much He wants to share; therefore beloved, Be Still in Him and know He is God.

Listen...Your name is being called by the most loving voice your spirit can hear. <3

Lord, you are so very good. Draw me deeply into your presence where I experience your goodness. Father God cultivate my spirit to receive your father heart for me. I need you beyond words. Heal deep spaces that are unreconciled to your wholeness and holiness as my Father God. Lord, your presence is everything I need. May I feast with you, may I lay my head on your chest and savour your heart beating in my ears, and may I be transfigured by your presence that I live with the brightest afterglow. Lord you are so personal – speak to my spirit your desire for me to sit at your feet, savouring every moment. Draw me deeper, Lord. I ask all of this in your most intimate, knowing name, amen.

References;
NIV Bible
Commentary from Charles R. Wale Jr.'s voice recording on mercy; Arthur Burk

Invitation

Thank you for joining me on this journey; seeking, hearing, and discovering the depths of love available for each one of us. My prayer is that you have met with the heart of your Father, the love of the Son, and the fullness of the Holy Spirit as each word rose up to meet you, beloved. As I shared at the beginning, there is much to glean from each devotional, and there are still layers of goodness to discover. Journal, pray, and worship your way through these pages once again. He is so for you and delights in you. You are His beloved.

Lord we cannot thank you enough for simply being you. You are more than enough, your presence is what we profoundly desire; we are your good idea, we are your beloved. Draw us in deeply, Lord. We are loved because you are Love. You love us, you love us, you love us, you love us because that is who you are. Praise you forever, for there is no higher name. In the name of love, amen.

Afterword

This has been an experience far beyond intellect, far beyond knowledge. It has been a journey of "reveal your heart to me, give me eyes to see, lead me each step, teach me, I wait for you, Lord." This is but a sliver of the immense detail of each person's original design and our fullness in Christ. Oh, what a privilege to get a glimpse into the Father's heart for His crowning creation. We are truly amazing, my friends, because the creator, sculptor, and fulfiller of His heart in us, is exquisite.

To repeat my sentiments from the beginning, this work does not describe these gifts but is merely a humble attempt to speak to the heart of each one. Knowing full well that Jesus is cultivating all of Himself in us, so we too can hear with ears of all seven. The layers of God's heart, character, and design are so beautiful. The richness of each gift is only the beginning of the full inheritance promise for each person. God's love is lavish and endless.

I am honoured to be witness to and a part of it all.

God bless you richly,
Wendy Landin

Acknowledgments

I am so eternally grateful that the God of all, in all and overall, also had His heart set on mine. Without His love for me I would be a shell of His original design in me. Thank you Lord above all for simply everything, I am forever yours. <3

To my husband, Kevin, who has championed me, stood in the gap, and always spoken truth over me in the form of word and deed. You have saved me from myself countless times and your gospel simplicity fills in all the unity spaces between us. (He doesn't realize how prophetic he is but I do.) Love you forever, honeybunches. <3

To my children, Steven, Brittney, and son-in-law Mitchell. You are my greatest "get to" and I thank God for you every day! I love you like no other. I joyfully hold space for you and with you. I stand with you, I witness you, I see your hearts after the Lord's heartbeat, and I pray you forever catch His breath in you. You are a gift of heavenly goodness, and I am inspired by you every day. I forever choose you. <3

To one of the greatest artists I have ever met, Mitchell, ATRON Studios. You sir are gifted, talented and truly generous with your creative process and inspiration. You have created the most beautiful cover from only my vague yet sure directives. Thank you for bringing your willingness and belief in this project to create a masterpiece. I would choose you and your artistry a million times over. <3

To my sweet sisters in Christ, you my dears are Kingdom jewels. Your insight, wisdom, encouragement, and belief in what God is up to in me is valuable beyond measure. You don't know how profound you each are. Thank you for walking humbly before the Lord as I am a recipient of that overflow. Words fall short to describe how much you mean to me – I love you. <3

To those who the Lord saw fit to bring into my life. You are a treasure chest of goodness. You walk with me, you talk with me, and I hear God's voice through yours. You mean the world to me! I love the Lord even more for giving me the gift of you in my life. <3

To my fellow journeyer, as you read this book know that I had you in mind as I typed out each word – I have said a thousand prayers for you. God sees you, He knows you, and He is so for you. You fully belong and are His Beloved. May this experience be as precious to you as it has been for me. Blessings. <3

About the Author

Wendy Landin has walked intimately with Jesus as her Lord for over two decades. Years ago, she discovered that her greatest passion was cultivating spaces where people could encounter the living God and engage with the freedom He provides. This led to many ministries as well as entering the fitness industry which cultivates relationships with women in a safe, intimate environment that brings positive outcomes.

Wendy is a speaker, personal trainer, group fitness instructor and she has created a wellness/weight loss course, which was born out of her own redemptive health journey. She has her Master Holy Yoga instructor certification, trauma-sensitive training, and is the Canadian Shepherd/Soul Care provider for the Holy Yoga Foundation. Wendy lives in Innisfail, Alberta with her husband Kevin and favorite feline, Shadow. They have two adult children, Steven and Brittney, and son-in-law, Mitchell. Her family is the greatest get-to of her life. God has the best ideas.

Join Wendy at www.youaremybeloved.ca, follow on Instagram, Twitter and find her on Facebook.

Insta; @wendyslandin
FB @WendyLandin
Twitter @wendyslandin

Printed in Canada